COMMUNITY WORKERS

Delivering Your Mail

A Book About Mail Carriers

Ann Owen

Illustrated by Eric Thomas

Thanks to our advisers for their expertise, research, knowledge, and advice:

Sarah Wyatt, United States Postal Service, Mound, Minnesota

Susan Kesselring, M.A., Literacy Educator
Rosemount-Apple Valley-Eagan (Minnesota) School District

PICTURE WINDOW BOOKS
Minneapolis, Minnesota

Managing Editor: Bob Temple
Creative Director: Terri Foley
Editor: Peggy Henrikson
Editorial Adviser: Andrea Cascardi
Copy Editor: Laurie Kahn
Designer: John Moldstad
Page production: Picture Window Books
The illustrations in this book were prepared digitally.

Picture Window Books
1710 Roe Crest Drive
North Mankato, MN 56003
www.capstonepub.com

Library of Congress Cataloging-in-Publication Data
Owen, Ann, 1953–
Delivering your mail : a book about mail carriers / written by Ann Owen ; illustrated by Eric Thomas.
p. cm. — (Community workers)
Summary: Describes some of the things that letter carriers do to make sure
people in the community get their mail.
Includes bibliographical references and index.
ISBN-13: 978-1-4048-0091-5 (library binding)
ISBN-10: 1-4048-0091-3 (library binding)
ISBN-13: 978-1-4048-0485-2 (paperback)
ISBN-10: 1-4048-0485-4 (paperback)
1. Letter carriers—United States—Juvenile literature.
[1. Letter carriers. 2. Occupations.] I. Thomas, Eric, ill.
II. Title. III. Community workers (Picture Window Books)
HE6499 .O94 2004
383'.4973—dc21
                                                         2003004582

Many people
in your community
have jobs helping others.

What do mail carriers do?

Mail carriers sort the mail

and deliver it.

The mail carrier delivers letters and even birthday presents.

Are you Susan?

Mail carriers always make sure the mail gets to the right place.

The mail carrier delivers your valentines

and brings you some, too.

A mail carrier drives a truck
with a steering wheel
on the same side as the curb.

Mail carriers walk from house to house

and store to store.

A mail carrier drives through snow

and sometimes walks in the rain.

The mail carrier always follows a route.

Mail carriers go to homes in the city

and farms in the country.

19

Everywhere, mail carriers deliver the mail.

Did You Know?

Mail carriers stop and go a lot, and they can't always see all the way around their vehicles. To be safe, don't get too close to a delivery vehicle. Wait until the carrier is gone to get your mail.

Most vehicles have the steering wheel on the left side, but post office delivery vehicles have the steering wheel on the right. Then the mail carrier can easily reach out the window and put mail in the mailboxes.

About 150 years ago, young Pony Express riders delivered mail from Missouri to California. Each rider went about 75 miles, changing horses six or seven times. Then the rider handed off the mail to the next rider.

Mail carriers have to use snowmobiles or boats to deliver mail to some people who live on islands or in remote areas.

Mail Throughout the Years

When	What	How Long Ago
27 B.C.	The Romans had a great mail system, but it was just for government people. Most people didn't know how to read back then.	2,030 years
1639	Before the United States was even a country, the first post office in America opened in Boston, Massachusetts. It was in someone's home.	More than 360 years
1775	Benjamin Franklin was named the first postmaster general.	About 230 years
1840	The world's first postage stamp was created in Great Britain. It had a picture of Queen Victoria on it.	About 160 years
1860	The Pony Express service began.	More than 140 years
1918	Airplanes started carrying mail across the country on a regular basis.	More than 85 years

Words to Know

community (kuh-MYOO-nuh-tee) – a group of people who live in the same area

deliver (di-LIV-ur) – to take something to a place or a person

postage stamp (POH-stij STAMP) – a sticker that you put on your mail to show you have paid to have it delivered

post office (POHST OFF-iss) – the place where people can buy stamps and mail letters or packages. Mail carriers go to the post office to pick up the mail they deliver.

route (ROUT) – a particular way to go or series of places to visit. A mail carrier's route is where the carrier goes to deliver mail every day.

vehicle (VEE-uh-kuhl) – something used to carry people or things from place to place. A mail carrier's delivery vehicle is usually a truck or car.

To Learn More

At the Library

Flanagan, Alice K. *Letter Carriers*. Minneapolis: Compass Point Books, 2000.

Harness, Cheryl. *They're Off! The Story of the Pony Express*. New York: Simon & Schuster Books for Young Readers, 1996.

Ready, Dee. *Mail Carriers*. Mankato, Minn.: Bridgestone Books, 1998.

Schaefer, Lola M. *We Need Mail Carriers*. Mankato, Minn.: Pebble Books, 2000.

Skurzynski, Gloria. *Here Comes the Mail*. New York: Bradbury Press, 1992.

On the Web

FactHound offers a safe, fun way to find Web sites related to topics in this book. All of the sites on FactHound have been researched by our staff.

1. Visit *www.facthound.com*
2. Type in this special code: 1404800913
3. Click on the FETCH IT button.

Your trusty FactHound will fetch the best sites for you!

Index